Bull Whackers to Whistle Punks

Logging in the Old West

BULL WHACKERS
to
WHISTLE PUNKS

LOGGING IN THE OLD WEST

by SHARLENE and TED NELSON

FRANKLIN WATTS

A Division of Grolier Publishing

NEW YORK   LONDON   HONG KONG   SYDNEY
DANBURY, CONNECTICUT

To Calvin and Carlie and their great-grandfather DeWitt Nelson.

NOTE TO READERS: Words in bold are new terms defined in the glossary. Words in italics are new terms defined in the main text.

Cover photograph copyright ©: Special Collections Division, University of Washington Libraries (UW11843)

Photographs copyright ©: Special Collections Division, University of Washington Libraries: pp. 2 (UW121580), 30 (UW14407), 40 (UW25), 43 (UW11835), 49 (UW6581), 52 (UW11843); Vantage Art: p. 8; North Wind Picture Archives: pp. 38, 39; D. Kinsey Collection, Whatcom Museum of History and Art, Bellingham, WA: pp. 12, 20, 34, 45; Oregon Historical Society: pp. 10 (ORHI91693), 16 (ORHI92852), 24 (ORHI59850), 26 (ORHI13303), 36 (ORHI52198), 55 (ORHI92853); Link and Pin Museum: p. 18; The Bettmann Archive: p. 19; Coyle Turner Collection: p. 29; Washington State Historical Society: p. 51; Weyerhaeuser Company: p. 57.

Library of Congress Cataloging-in-Publication Data

Nelson, Sharlene P.
Bull whackers to whistle punks : logging in the Old West / by
Sharlene and Ted Nelson.
p. cm. — (A First book)
Includes bibliographical references and index.
Summary: Details the lives and innovations of nineteenth-century loggers
in the Old West including a look at the language they created.
ISBN 0-531-20228-3
1. Logging—West (U.S.)—History—19th century—Juvenile
literature. 2. Loggers—West (U.S.)—History—19th century—
Juvenile literature. 3. Logging—West (U.S.)—Terminology—
Juvenile literature. 4. Loggers—West (U.S.)—Language—Juvenile
literature. [1. Logging—West (U.S.) 2. Loggers —West (U.S.)]
I. Nelson, Ted W. II. Title. III. Series.
SD538.2.W4N45 1996
634.9'8'0978—dc20   95-48907 CIP AC

CONTENTS

PROLOGUE

This is the story of the loggers who worked in the **forests** of the West from the 1850s until the early 1900s. They brought logs to sawmills with oxen goaded by the **bull whacker's** stick and later with powerful steam engines that roared into action at the **whistle punk's** signal. Lumber sawed from the logs helped build a nation.

Their story begins in 1848 when James Marshall found gold while building a sawmill in the foothills of California's Sierra Nevada mountains. His discovery led to the California Gold Rush, and thousands of people trekked west to seek fortunes in the shining metal. Others came seeking gold of another kind. These men knew that lumber would be needed to build homes, stores, hotels, saloons, churches, and docks. When they arrived, there were only a few sawmills, but they found vast forests of evergreen trees that were ideal for making lumber.

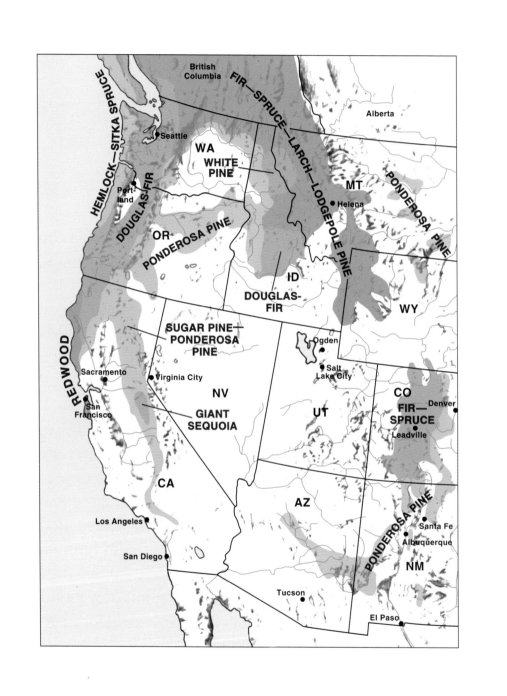

A forest of Douglas-fir grew on the west side of the Cascade Range, in present-day Washington and Oregon, and along the Coast Mountains of British Columbia. East of the Cascades a ponderosa pine forest thrived, and from southern Oregon down the Sierra Nevada mountains stretched a forest of sugar pine and ponderosa pine. Redwoods stood along California's north coast, and giant sequoias towered in the southern Sierras. Other kinds of trees grew in forests along the coast of the Pacific Northwest, on the high plateaus and mountains of the Southwest, and in the Rockies.

At the edge of the Douglas-fir and redwood forests, the gold-rush lumbermen began building sawmills and hiring loggers to bring the logs in. The first loggers were ship deserters, early settlers, and unsuccessful gold miners. Later, as sawmills were built throughout the West, many loggers came from Sweden, Norway, Finland, and the forests of the Lake States and eastern Canada.

A map showing the forests of the western United States and southwestern Canada. Shades of green indicate different forest types.

The loggers brought logs to sawmills, such as this one on
California's redwood coast. Here the logs were sawed into
lumber, loaded on ships, and then delivered to market.
Lumber sawed at inland mills could not be transported by sea.
It was delivered locally by wagon, and after the railroad came
to the forest, it was carried longer distances by trains.

Loggers were a tough breed. They lived in remote camps and worked ten to twelve hours a day, six days a week, in rain, snow, and mud, or heat and dust. Their work was dangerous. But, despite the rigors and risks, they would rather log than do anything else.

Loggers were innovators, too. They devised tools to help fall giant trees. As logging moved deeper into the forests, they invented and adapted methods and machinery to move huge logs over long distances, often across rugged terrain.

They spoke a language that grew to several thousand words and phrases, most of which could only be understood by other loggers. When strung together, the words and phrases had a lilt, almost a music like the cowboys' songs.

After reading their story, you'll know what happened to an injured logger who described his accident when he finally reached the hospital. He told the nurse, "I was setting chokers and was just hooking up to a big blue butt when the rigging slinger yelled, 'Ho,' to the punk. The punk jerked the wire, the puncher opened 'er wide, and well, here I am."

Some western trees were large enough to become a family home, such as this hollowed-out cedar in western Washington.

LOGGERS
on
SPRINGBOARDS

1

The West's first loggers were like David, dwarfed by the Goliath trees. The trees were among of the largest on earth. The oldest had been growing for three thousand years.

Their size was made legendary by stories and pictures. One story described thirty-two people dancing on the stump of one tree, and an old etching showed a horse and rider turning inside a log hollowed out by fire. A painting showed a wagon road tunneled through the base of a growing tree.

Stories and pictures like these were only novelties to the loggers. They thought of trees in the practical terms of their diameter, the tree's height to its top, and the distance to the first limb. The largest trees measured 17 to 32 feet (5 to 10 m) in diameter near their base and reached over 300 feet (90 m) toward the sky. The first limb might be 150 feet (45 m) above the ground. Trees 6 to 8 feet (2 to 2½ m) in diameter and 250 feet (76 m) tall were common.

Like David, the earliest loggers took on their task with tools of slingshot size. To cut down the trees they swung single-blade axes, chopping notches into the tree from two sides at its base and falling it in the direction of the lean. Once on the ground, the tree was cut into logs with crude saws.

Double-blade axes were developed in the late 1870s. Long **crosscut saws,** known to loggers as *misery whips,* were developed in the 1880s. With these improved tools a ritual evolved for falling trees and making logs.

The ritual began with two **fallers** and sometimes helpers. They carried axes, **springboards,** a crosscut saw, a sledgehammer, a sack full of steel wedges, an old whiskey bottle filled with oil, a bottle of water, and their lunches in a cloth sack or tin bucket.

At the tree to be cut they cleared brush and small trees and cut escape paths away from its base. Then, with an ax handle held between thumb and forefinger, they sighted up the tree to help determine the direction of fall.

With a careful eye they looked for dangers such as *widow makers*, limbs that could break away as the tree fell and crush a faller below. Then they walked the ground where the tree would fall. There was no sense in working hours or even days to fall a tree and have it shatter on rocks, downed trees, or **stumps** hidden in the brush.

Next they set the springboards, planks 4 to 6 feet (1 to 2 m) long with a sharp metal lip bolted to one end. They jammed the lip into a notch chopped in the tree so the springboard would stick out of the trunk, parallel to the ground. Standing on the springboards the fallers could work above the tree's enlarged base. On larger trees the fallers might go up "two or three boards," or 8 to 12 feet (2½ to 3½ m) above the ground.

Like all loggers, the fallers wore *corked shoes.* These were laced boots with small steel spikes in the soles and heels. The spikes bit into the springboards as the loggers began to rhythmically chop the *undercut,* a

notch facing the direction in which the tree would fall. Chips larger than a hand flew in the air as the undercut gradually took shape.

When the undercut reached about one-third into the tree, the fallers exchanged their axes for the two-man crosscut saw. On the side of the tree opposite the notch they began the *backcut*. As the fallers pushed and pulled the saw, a metallic, ringing sound echoed in the **woods.** They paused. One of the men reached for the bottle hanging on a wire hook and dashed oil on the saw to clear the blade of *pitch,* the tree's sticky resin. As the blade bit deeper, the fallers alternately sawed and sledgehammered wedges into the cut to help tip the tree.

With the backcut nearly finished, one faller shouted a warning, "Timmberr... down the hill!" A few more blows on the wedges and the tree's top began to waver. A few more strokes of the saw, and the tree began to tip.

Loggers took pride in falling trees in an exact direction. This faller sights along the handle of his ax, placed in the undercut, to be sure the tree will fall where intended.

(above) With the undercut finished, fallers lean into the long crosscut saw to begin the backcut in a Sitka spruce.

(right) The backcut is nearly finished and the fallers use steel wedges and sledgehammers to help tip a Douglas-fir.

A bucker saws the first, or butt log, from a Douglas-fir. To keep
the saw from binding, he is bucking upward from the
underside of the tree. His saw is supported on a metal arm.

There was a brief silence, then a crack as wood
between the notch and the backcut began to break. The
fallers leaped from their springboards and ran to safety.
There was a groan as fiber pulled from the stump, a
whoosh, and finally a ground-shaking crash.

A *bucker* followed. Working alone, he measured and then marked with an ax where he would cut the fallen tree into logs. The lengths marked depended on the sawmill's needs and varied from 16 to more than 40 feet (5 to 12 m). Only logs with the fewest limbs were selected.

The lonely bucker then began sawing with his long crosscut saw. He also used wedges to keep the cuts open and oil to clean the pitch from the saw. On steep ground he worked from the uphill side. A careless bucker could be crushed by a log suddenly rolling downhill. He chopped limbs, some as large as small trees, from the logs and then moved on.

In the early days of logging other men often followed. They stripped bark from the logs and **sniped** the ends to ease the log's ride over the ground. Then the logs were ready to be transported to the sawmill.

BULL WHACKER'S SHOUT

2

At dawn, a bull whacker and the camp's **bull cook** began **yoking** up the oxen. To the loggers, the oxen were bulls. To the bull whacker, each bull had a name: Big Red, Spot, Whitey. When yoked together in pairs, with the bull whacker at their side, the bulls began plodding up a gently sloping *skidroad*.

Built earlier, the skidroad was a broad roadway through the woods. It wound past stumps and beneath trees left standing that were too small for the sawmill or unsuitable for lumber. Small trees had been felled

perpendicular to the roadway at intervals. With their limbs and bark removed and lying half buried in the muddy ground, they formed the road's skids.

About 1 mile (1½ km) into the woods the bull whacker turned his bulls around, then nudged them backward toward five logs that lay on the skidroad, one behind the other. The logs had been rolled or dragged to the skidroad, one at a time, by loggers using huge **jacks** or a few bulls.

The *hooktender* hammered hooks into the first log in line. It was the first and biggest log from the tree, called the *butt,* or blue butt if especially heavy. Iron chains leading from these hooks were connected to the bulls' yokes. More hooks with short chains connected the other logs together in a row behind the butt.

When the hooktender signaled that all was ready, the bull whacker gave a shout. The bulls leaned forward. Chains clanked as they tightened against the first log. Once moving, its momentum would help pull the other logs. The bulls bellowed, and the yokes creaked.

At first there was only noise and little forward progress. The bull whacker shouted even louder. His goad stick flashed against bulls' rumps and shoulders. The *skid greaser,* a teenage boy learning the logger's trade, darted behind the hooves of the last pair of bulls.

Bulls move down a skidroad beneath the bull whacker's raised goad stick. The skid greaser, with a tin of grease over his shoulder, darts to safety as the logs slide by.

He carried a bucket of grease and swabbed the skids to ease the friction. Slowly, the logs began to move.

Now the bull whacker used the skill that made him one of the highest paid loggers. Driving the bulls too fast on a gradual turn could cause a log to lunge for-

ward. A valued bull could be crushed, only to become meat for the cookhouse table. Too slow and the procession would come to a stop.

With his shouting, prodding, and cajoling, the bull whacker artfully guided the bulls to the skidroad's end. The logs were unhooked, and he turned his bulls around. With the hooks and chains dragging behind, the bulls headed back up the skidroad for more logs.

The earliest skidroads led directly to sawmills. As logging moved farther into the forest, skidroads ended at a *landing,* a collection point for logs on their way to the mill. From landings on beaches, the logs were rolled into the water and then towed to the mills by boats. Some landings were at the head of chutes where logs hurtled down steep hills into water below.

Today, modern skyscrapers in Vancouver, British Columbia, in Seattle, Washington, and in Portland, Oregon, tower above busy streets that once were skidroads. The rush of cars and buses has replaced the slow plodding of the bull whacker's bulls.

In the era of animal logging, some loggers preferred more agile horses to bulls. In the drier climates and gentler terrain of the inland pine forests, teams of horses pulled wagons loaded with logs. They also used *big wheels.* These were two wooden, spoked wheels 10

Big wheels, with ponderosa pine logs suspended beneath, are pulled by a team of horses. The lever extending above the axle acts as a hoisting device to raise or lower the front end of the logs.

to 12 feet (3 to 3½ m) in diameter. With the front end of the logs suspended beneath the axle, clouds of dust billowed as the the horse-drawn wheels rolled ahead.

Still other early loggers used muscle power and water to move logs to the sawmills. They pumped or turned heavy, long-handled jacks to push and roll logs into bays, rivers, and streams. Often, they had to wait for winter **freshets** to float their logs to the mill.

DONKEY POWER

3

While bulls and horses were straining at their loads, John Dolbeer was thinking about another way to move logs. Before becoming a sawmiller and a logger in the redwoods, Dolbeer had been a seafarer. He remembered the little deck-mounted steam engines used on ships to hoist anchors and raise cargoes. Because they produced less than one horsepower, they were called *donkey engines* or, simply, donkeys.

In 1881 Dolbeer mounted a donkey on a wooden **sled** and moved it into the woods. Bull whackers watched with amused disdain as Dolbeer hooked a rope leading from the little engine to a big redwood log. More wood was thrown into the firebox beneath the donkey's boiler. Dolbeer pushed the throttle forward. In less time than it took a bull whacker to turn a team of bulls, the log was pulled to the donkey. Dolbeer patented his invention a year later, and the age of steam logging began.

The boilers of the first donkeys stood upright, about as tall as a man. They had a smokestack that looked like an upside-down funnel. Steam powered a small piston attached to a geared shaft that turned a vertical spool. The donkey's wooden sled was tied to stumps to hold it in place.

A horse, called a *line horse*, pulled a thick manila rope from the donkey out to a log. The hooktender set hooks attached to the end of the manila rope into one end of the log. A *spool tender* wrapped several loops of the rope around the donkey's spool. He pulled hard on the rope to keep the loops from slipping. The *donkey puncher*, puncher for short, pushed the throttle all the way forward, "opening 'er wide," as the loggers said. Steam and smoke spewed. Sparks flew. As the spool turned, the rope wound in, and the log moved forward.

At first the donkeys could pull logs only a short

An early donkey and logging crew: the line horse is ready to pull the line and hook out to the logs, and the donkey puncher stands near the boiler. The spool tender has coiled the line around the donkey's spool.

distance. Bulls or horses took over for the long pulls. But loggers were always looking for bigger and better ways to do things. They began to improve on Dolbeer's idea.

By the 1890s the boilers were bigger and the engines more powerful, though they were still called donkeys. They featured steel cables that wound around

Bigger donkeys, with horizontal drums, gradually replaced the first donkeys. The forward drum holds the mainline that pulls the logs in. The drum behind holds the haulback that pulls the mainline back out to the logs.

two horizontal drums like fishing line winds on a reel. One drum held the *mainline,* a thick cable that pulled the logs in. The second drum held a smaller cable, called the *haulback.* It was threaded through **blocks** secured to distant stumps and then connected to the mainline's end, forming a loop leading 1,000 feet (305 m) or more into the woods. After the mainline had pulled the logs in, the haulback, which replaced the plodding line horses, returned the mainline to where more logs lay.

Pulling logs along the ground with donkeys became known as *ground lead logging*. Now the hooktender reigned supreme. He knew where to place the donkey to pull in the most logs in the shortest time. He knew where to place blocks along the mainline to guide logs around trees and stumps. His helper, the rigging slinger, told the *chokermen* where to set the *chokers*—iron chains and, later, steel cables that were wrapped around a log and hooked to the mainline. The rigging slinger also told the whistle punk what to signal to the donkey puncher.

The whistle punk, or punk for short, like the skid greaser, was usually a young boy learning the logger's trade. He strung a wire from a steam whistle on the donkey through the woods to the place where the chokermen were working. When the whistle punk jerked the wire, the whistle tooted. Different combinations of long and short toots were like a code between the rigging slinger and donkey puncher.

A whistle punk strings his jerk wire from the donkey to where the rigging slinger and chokermen will work.

When the rigging slinger shouted, "Ho," the whistle punk jerked the wire once, the whistle tooted, and the donkey puncher opened 'er wide. The donkey let out resounding chugs as the logs thundered over the ground. When the logs reached the donkey, the chokers were unhooked, and the haulback pulled the main-line and chokers back into the woods.

There was a brief pause. Steam hissed from the idling donkey. The fireman's ax thunked as he split wood for the donkey's firebox. The chokermen grunted and strained to set chokers around more logs. When the rigging slinger shouted, the whistle punk jerked the wire, and the whistle echoed through the woods. The donkey chugged, and logs crashed ahead again.

When logging in an area was finished, it was moving day. The hooktender and his crew led the donkey's cables through a block tied to a distant stump. Instead of pulling logs, the donkey pulled itself. The puncher worked the throttle with one hand and held on with the other. The donkey, on its wooden sled, lurched forward around stumps and over logs.

As the donkeys became more powerful, some loggers used them instead of bulls and horses on the long skidroad pulls. Several donkeys were set up along a skidroad thousands of feet apart. Long lines of logs

"Off to see Aunt Mary," or moving day: a donkey on its wooden sled with its cable attached to a distant stump, pulls itself to a new logging site. A crude log bridge helps ease the ride over an obstacle.

pulled by the donkeys' cables were relayed from donkey to donkey. But other loggers were finding an even better way to move logs long distances. Railroads were coming to the forests.

LOGGING
with
LOKIES

4

About the time they started using donkeys, a few loggers were beginning to lay rails to where the donkeys, bulls, or horses worked. Little steam locomotives, called *lokies* by the loggers, puffed along the rails carrying logs bound for the sawmills. Moving logs long distances on railroads became a challenge to the logger's creativity and the blacksmith's skill.

Some loggers made their own locomotives with wooden sleds mounted on wheels powered by donkey engines. Others brought discarded steam trolley cars from cities and put them to work in the woods.

This homemade lokie, which has no brakes, drags a load of logs along the railroad ties. Rocks are placed between the rails to slow the logs' descent and keep them from overtaking the lokie as they are pulled downhill.

Early loggers built their railroads with simple tools: picks and shovels, wheelbarrows, dynamite, and metal scoops dragged by bulls or horses. They laid rails on wooden ties over rough ground and up steep grades. Sharp turns twisted around obstacles.

Except where close to the sawmill, the railroads were usually temporary. Expensive iron rails had to be picked up for use elsewhere. Rails made from peeled poles or sawed timbers that could be left behind were often laid in place of iron rails. Log bridges spanned streams and gullies.

Many of the loggers' first locomotives had drive wheels powered by rods connected directly to the engine's pistons. They worked best on gentle grades. In the 1880s, manufacturers began producing locomotives especially for logging. Their drive wheels were connected to the pistons by gears and geared shafts. They could climb steep grades and roll around sharp curves on rails spaced only 3 feet (90 cm) apart.

There were several ways to haul logs along the railroads. Some engines dragged logs on planks laid between the rails. Flat cars were used, but they were heavy and too short to carry long logs. Long logs were hauled on *trucks,* which were rectangular wooden frames with a railroad wheel at each corner. One truck supported the front end of a load of logs, one supported the back end. Together, the trucks and logs formed a railroad car.

At first, loading logs onto the cars or trucks or between the rails was a slow task. At the loading point, the loggers laid log skids perpendicular to the rails. The logs were rolled along the skids and into place by men using jacks or **peaveys**, or with long chains pulled by bulls or horses.

In the mid 1890s, loggers began using donkeys to roll the logs into place. A cable from the donkey's drum was threaded through blocks, laid beneath a log on the skids, and then secured to a nearby stump. When the donkey's drum turned, the cable tightened against the underside of the log, and the log rolled down the skids with ease.

Now the sights and sounds of logging were chang-

A train loaded with redwood logs on its way to the sawmill

ing from the bull whacker's days. Locomotives rolled to where two donkeys were hissing steam. One was pulling logs from the woods, the other rolling logs onto the train. When the train was loaded, the locomotive's whistle sounded a mournful counterpoint to the shrill toots of the whistle punk's signal. Smoke billowed as the fireman threw more wood into the locomotive's firebox. The train gathered speed. The engine began to sway along the rough tracks. On steep downgrades, brakemen scurried over the loads of logs and set the brakes by hand to slow the rumbling train.

Loggers pose for a picture before going into the cookhouse.
This remote camp, like others, was used for a short time and
then abandoned when loggers moved to a new area.

LIFE
in the
CAMPS

5

The loggers' home was a camp deep in the forest miles from town. Crude wooden buildings stood in a clearing: bunkhouses, a shack for the timekeeper, a blacksmith's shop, barns for the bulls or horses, a cookhouse, and, in the railroad days, sheds for the locomotives.

Most loggers were bachelors. When they arrived in camp, they carried their few possessions in a bedroll. Packed inside were slippers, a change of socks and long underwear, a box of soap, a toothbrush, and a razor and strap. Corked shoes were tied outside. A pipe or a tin of chewing tobacco was stuffed into a pants pocket.

When a logger arrived, he hoped to claim a top bunk from the narrow, wooden beds stacked along the bunkhouse walls. Mattresses were often made from tree boughs, and as they dried, the needlelike leaves fell on the sleepers below. Cloth mattresses came later, but they attracted bedbugs.

The logger's day began before sunrise when the logging boss yelled, "Daylight in the swamp." The men stumbled from their bunks clothed in long woolen underwear that they wore day and night year round. Over their underwear, each logger pulled on a wool shirt, pants and suspenders, then socks and slippers. Corked shoes were not allowed in the cookhouse.

Outside, some splashed cold water on their faces from tin basins. Others gathered near the cookhouse door. All savored the smell of frying bacon and wood smoke from the cookhouse stove. It was a welcome change from the bunkhouse smells of sweat, tobacco, drying socks, and long underwear.

The cook's helper clanged a metal triangle hanging next to the cookhouse, and the men filed inside. Tables were set with plates of steaming pork chops, gravy and biscuits, hotcakes, bacon and ham, fried potatoes, and pots of coffee.

Always sitting in the same place, the men ate qui-

The camp cook (left) and his helper (right) cook and bake
to satisfy the loggers' huge appetites. Loggers ate double
and sometimes triple servings of meat, vegetables, potatoes,
biscuits with butter, cakes, and pies but never gained weight.

etly. Only the sounds of forks clinking on crockery
plates or, "Pass the syrup," "Pass the coffee," could be
heard. When finished, the men usually packed their
own lunch at a table stacked with meat, bread slices,
and cake. Back at the bunkhouse they laced up their

corked shoes, then headed for the woods. Early loggers walked. In later years they rode on railroad flatcars.

During the day the cook spent most of his time preparing the evening meal. His helper washed the dishes, set them out on the oilcloth-covered tables for the next meal, and swept the cookhouse floor. The bull cook chopped wood for the stoves and fed leftovers to the pigs. He hauled water in buckets from a nearby stream where meat, jugs of milk, and vegetables were stored to keep cool.

Toward evening the loggers returned. They removed their corked shoes, hung wet socks and long underwear over the bunkhouse rafters, and washed in the tin basins. The cookhouse triangle clanged, and the hungry men filed into the cookhouse. They sat down at tables laden with hot food and sometimes a special treat—pies made from wild berries picked that day by the cook's helper.

After dinner the men returned to the bunkhouse and stoked up a potbellied stove in the room's center. By the dim light of a lantern, they played cards and swapped stories.

The camp's cook and his food were always a topic of bunkhouse conversations. Meals were one of the loggers' few pleasures. If the food was good, the loggers

Bunkhouses were small, their furnishings simple: wood benches and wood bunk beds. Often thirty to forty loggers lived in one bunkhouse. There was only enough space to read a book, write letters, play cards, or sleep.

stayed. If the meals were poor or skimpy, grim-faced loggers rolled up their blankets and moved on to another camp.

Sunday was the loggers' day off. They patched and washed their underwear and socks, and trimmed each other's hair and moustaches. It was a day of rest for the loggers, but not for the cook. As usual, he was busy preparing meals.

After months of enduring the camp's isolation, the loggers looked forward to the Fourth of July. Next to Christmas, this was the biggest holiday of the year. The men drew their wages from the timekeeper and headed for town. In town, gambling halls, saloons, and dance halls were sparkling clean and decorated with red, white, and blue banners. All were attractions to help the loggers celebrate and spend their money. Three days later, the loggers returned to camp with empty pockets, ready to work again and earn wages for their next trip to town.

In railroad logging days, some camps were portable. Bunkhouses, offices, and the cookhouse, each the size of a train's boxcar, were mounted on wheels. When logging moved to a new area, it was moving day for the *car camp*. Hooked up behind a locomotive, the camp rolled over tracks to a new clearing in the woods.

HIGHBALL LOGGING

6

By the early 1900, logging had grown far beyond its gold-rush roots. Lumber from western sawmills was being shipped around the world. Bulls and horses were still working, but steam was becoming the dominant power.

Railroads were pushing deeper into the forests. Pile-driving donkeys were building high railroad **trestles** across deep canyons. Steam donkeys, on sleds or mounted on rail cars, were powerful enough to lift logs onto trains.

Rivers, impounded behind splash dams, held hundreds of logs. When the dam's gates were opened, the logs surged downriver. In the northern Rockies, loggers drove logs down long rivers swollen with melting snow. Big wheels pulled logs through the pine forest of the Southwest.

Still, the loggers kept looking for more efficient ways to bring in the logs. In forests of the Northwest they soon mastered the art of *high lead logging*. Just as Dolbeer's donkey had come from a ship's engine, the idea for high lead logging came from the rigging on a ship's mast. It relied on the heavy and powerful donkeys of the day, and the daring *high climbers*.

A tree near the railroad, and 4 to 5 feet (1 to 1½ m) in diameter at its base, was selected to become a **spar tree.** The first high climbers went up the spar tree on two springboards. Standing on one springboard, the logger chopped a notch above for the second board. When it was set, he scrambled up on it and pulled the first board after him. Springboard over springboard, the high climber went 60 to 80 feet (18 to 24 m) up the tree.

This slow and risky method soon gave way to high climbers with steel spurs. At the spar tree's base the high climber strapped the spurs to his corked shoes. He wrapped a rope around the tree and securely tied each end to his belt. With an upward flip of the rope and spurs digging into the tree's thick bark, he began to climb. An ax and saw dangled from his waist.

The high climber chopped or sawed away limbs as he went. When almost 200 feet (60 m) above the ground, he cut the top from the tree with ax and saw. When the top fell, the tree whipped in violent arcs, and he hung on tightly to his rope. When the tree steadied, the climber pulled himself up to its freshly cut top. From there he enjoyed a chew of tobacco and the view across forested slopes.

A small block was pulled up

A high climber, nearly 200 feet (60 m) above the ground, hangs on as the tree's top begins to fall.

the spar tree with a rope let down by the high climber. When secured, a light cable from the donkey's drum was threaded through the block. This line was used to pull bigger blocks, some weighing nearly a ton, and thick cables up the spar. When fully rigged, the spar tree became the center of an intricate web of cables and blocks. Each had a name and purpose known only to loggers.

Loggers still used a mainline pulled far into the woods by the haulback. But, unlike ground lead logging, the lines were held high in the air by blocks on the spar tree. When the lines were slacked, they dangled close to the ground. The rigging slinger and his crew set steel chokers around the logs and attached them to the mainline. On the whistle punk's signal, the mainline was tightened, and the ends of the logs were lifted off the ground and pulled. The logs nearly flew toward the spar tree.

This was the era of *highball logging*. Piles of logs stacked up around the spar tree's base. With more drums and cables added, the donkeys could pull logs to the spar tree and load logs onto rail cars at the same time. Each highball logger had a specific job and title, and as they sprang to work, the scene beneath the towering spar tree became frenzied.

A fully rigged spar tree towers above the loggers working below.

As the logs crashed onto the landing a *chaser* ran to release the chokers. The cables sang through the blocks as the chokers and mainline were hauled back to the woods. *Tong shakers* scrambled over the logs, pulling heavy tongs suspended from overhead cables. After the tongs were set, the logs were lifted and then dropped onto a rail car with a thick thump.

Far from the donkey, the chokermen struggled to set chokers around the logs. The donkey's whistle tooted repeatedly as the whistle punk jerked the wire in response to the rigging slinger's shouts.

It was a dangerous time. Logs could drop onto the tong shakers as tongs pulled loose. Logs could slip from the chokers and fall on the men below. Too often the donkey's whistle sounded seven long blasts, the signal that a logger was hurt. The lucky ones finished the season on crutches.

Around 1915, the loggers developed a bigger and better way to log with steam. They created the *tower skidder.* Traveling on rails and weighing nearly 250 tons (227 t), it carried its own "spar tree," a steel tower that

The tong shaker attaches heavy tongs to the logs. Then the logs are lifted to the train by the donkey behind.

could be raised and lowered. A steel boom extended forward for loading logs onto trains. When set up, the tower skidder was a maze of drums, cables, and blocks. With a mainline reaching 3,000 feet (915 m), it left a swath of stumps behind as it moved through the woods.

About this same time, gasoline engines were coming to the woods. Trucks with solid rubber wheels began to haul logs down plank roads. Power saws gradually replaced the fallers' crosscut saws. Tractors pulled logs where horses and bulls once worked.

The tower skidder's roar sounded the beginning of the end of steam logging in the Old West.

Tower skidders, like this one, were the last innovation in steam-logging equipment before gasoline, and later, diesel engines.

EPILOGUE

There are many reminders of logging in the Old West. Stumps with springboard notches still loom beneath tall **second-growth** trees. Loggers, wearing corked shoes, climb past them as they log again where the first loggers worked. Now their logs supply an array of products from lumber and paper to chemicals used in making football helmets and ice cream.

Fallers and buckers work with gasoline-powered chain saws. Portable steel towers, diesel powered and mounted on rubber tires, log where steam donkeys once worked. The whistle punk is extinct. Radio signals sent by the rigging slinger sound a horn that echoes through the woods. Rubber-tired diesel tractors pull logs where big wheels once rolled.

The railroads are gone, but diesel log trucks growl down logging roads built along an old railroad's path. Crumbling wooden trestles stand near modern bridges.

The logging camps are gone. Today's loggers live

at home. Still, bits of crockery, an oil bottle, and a rusting horseshoe can be found where a busy camp once stood.

But gone forever is the bull whacker's shout and the bellow of his bulls.

A modern steel tower harvests second-growth trees. Stumps from the first logging can be seen on the hillside. When the logging is completed, seedlings planted by hand will grow into a new forest.

GLOSSARY

Block	a metal case enclosing one or more pulleys. The pulleys increase the pulling and lifting power of a steel cable threaded through the block.
Bull cook	a logger who does odd jobs around a logging camp.
Bull whacker	a logger who guides teams of bulls pulling logs.
Crosscut saw	a saw with teeth that cut through the wood and pull shavings from the cut to keep the saw from binding.
Fallers	loggers who cut down trees. They were called choppers in the redwood forest.
Forest	a large area of trees, often named for the most frequently occurring kind of tree.

Freshet	a rise in a stream or river caused by heavy rains.
Jack	a mechanical device with large threads or ratchets worked by hand for moving logs short distances.
Peavey	a long-handled tool with a metal spiked point and a swinging metal hook near its end.
Second growth	a general term for trees that have grown back since previous logging.
Sled	a heavy frame with wooden runners on which a donkey sits.
Snipe	to round the edges of the front end of a log with an ax.
Spar tree	a tree, stripped of its branches and top, that is the center of an intricate system of cables and blocks used for high lead logging.
Springboard	a wooden plank 4 to 6 feet (1 to 2 m) long with a metal lip bolted to one end.
Stump	the base of a tree left standing after the tree is cut down.

Trestle	a braced framework of timbers or logs, called piles, that bridges a river or ravine.
Whistle punk	a logger who jerks a wire to sound a steam whistle signaling instructions to the donkey puncher.
Woods	a small area of trees within a forest—called bush in British Columbia.
Yoking	hitching bulls together by placing wooden frames, called yokes, around the animal's necks.

FURTHER READING

Adams, Peter D. *Early Loggers and the Sawmill.* New York: Crabtree Publishing Co., 1992.

Aylesworth, Thomas G. *The Northwest: Alaska, Idaho, Oregon, Washington.* New York: Chelsea House Publishers, 1988.

Bentley, Judith. *Railroad Workers and Loggers.* New York: 21st Century Books, Inc., 1995.

Gintzler, A. S. *Rough and Ready Loggers.* Santa Fe, N. Mex.: John Muir Publications, 1994.

Stone, Lynn M. *Timber Country.* Vero Beach, FL: Rourke Corp., 1993.

INDEX

ABOUT the AUTHORS

Sharlene and Ted Nelson are freelance writers living in the Pacific Northwest. Ted began his forty year career in the forest products industry marking log lengths for buckers still using crosscut saws. When first married, the couple lived in a northern California logging camp where Ted was resident forester.

They have written books about the Columbia and Snake rivers and the lighthouses of Washington, Oregon, and California. They have also written a history of Washington's forests for the state's middle schools. Their articles on regional history have been published in journals and magazines for travelers and children. This is their first book for Franklin Watts.

The couple has two married children and two grandchildren with whom they ski, sail, and backpack.